Winner of the L. E. Phillabaum Poetry Award for 2025

By Stone
and Needle

POEMS

Catherine W. Carter

LOUISIANA STATE UNIVERSITY PRESS
BATON ROUGE

Published by Louisiana State University Press
lsupress.org

Copyright © 2025 by Catherine W. Carter
All rights reserved. Except in the case of brief quotations used in articles or reviews, no part of this publication may be reproduced or transmitted in any format or by any means without written permission of Louisiana State University Press.

LSU Press Paperback Original

Designer: Kaelin Chappell Broaddus
Typefaces: Mrs Eves, dusplay; Filosofia, text.

Cover illustration Adobe Stock/ Shinpanu and 32 pixels

Cataloging-in-Publication Data are available from the Library of Congress.

ISBN 978-0-8071-8507-0 (pbk.: alk. paper) — ISBN 978-0-8071-8554-4 (pdf) — ISBN 978-0-8071-8553-7 (epub)

He hath his rihte cours forth holde
Be ston and nedle, til he cam
To Tharse, and there his lond he nam.

[He held onto his own true course
By stone and needle, till he came
To Tarsus, and made landfall there.]

—John Gower, *Confessio Amantis* 8.540–542,
trans. Brian Gastle and Catherine Carter

CONTENTS

    Acknowledgments xi

Grounding

    What magic is 3
    Witches' correspondences :: it's complicated 5
    Why I'm here 8
    Witch hairs 9
    In the hour of fire 10
    The broom closet 11
    When you know a witch's true name 12

East

    Butterflies, urine 15
    Can, worms 16
    The haunting 18
    Dupont Circle, skunk 20
    Willow minnows 21
    The neighborhoods of housewives 22
    Spring tonic 24

Southeast

    Lactobacilli 27
    This house 28
    The stars of love 30
    Artemis in Appalachia 31
    Earth says 34

South

    When you tell me I'm being racist   39
    Nail garden   41
    Ode: Candlefat   42
    In the plague year, I remember pinkeye   44
    Night sweat   46
    Earthflash   47

Southwest

    What time it is   51
    Campus, August evening, plague year   52
    The maidens of spring   54
    During the long meeting things begin to change: 55
    When you stop by High Noon for a new pierce   56
    Fuck: A blessing   57
    The change   58

The Earth Witch of Colchis

    Medea remembers the sheep   61
    Medea names herself   62
    But how could you kill the kids?   64

West

    Applesauce on the equinox   69
    Fat   71
    Ode: Slime   72
    Pre-menopausal red-tide death-period arrives while I walk with parents along Chesapeake beaches   74
    Aphrodite Ourania   75
    Ode: Erections in sleep   76
    Mountain brook lamprey   77
    The color of aquamarine: a spell for blessing   79
    Copperheads in heaven   80

Northwest

Four goldenrods   83
Things to love about the rain   84
Red beans   86
Until the cows come home   87
Elegy at All Hallows   88
Ode: Yeast   89
Sweet gum   91
At 50, my brother who always hated children finds a daughter   93

North

Winter solstice   97
Crow cosmogony   98
Ode: Anus   100
Happy light   101
The narrative of stones   102
Ode: Falafel   104
Cursive   105

Northeast

Pink red gold orange iridescent scarf   109
Red onion slices, salad bar, city hotel   110
The rivers run through you   112
Choptank bluegills take part in the creation of the world   114
Black wool coat on a hook   115

ACKNOWLEDGMENTS

Grateful acknowledgment is made to the editors and staffs of the following publications, in which the poems listed appeared previously, sometimes in slightly different form: *Artemis:* "Dupont circle, skunk"; *Asheville Poetry Review:* "Can, worms," "The change," and "Ode: Erections in sleep"; *Bay to Ocean Anthology,* Eastern Shore Writers' Network: "The rivers run through you," "Things to love about the rain", and "When you stop by High Noon for a new pierce"; *Cold Mountain Review:* "Copperheads in heaven," "Crow cosmogony," and "Nail garden"; *Delmarva Review:* "In the plague year, I remember pinkeye," "Red beans," "Red onions, salad bar, city hotel," "Sweet gum," and "Winter solstice"; *Ecotone:* "Earth says" and "Pre-Menopausal red-tide death-period arrives while I walk with parents along Chesapeake beaches"; *Good morning, unseen* (chapbook): "The color of aquamarine: a spell for blessing," "Lactobacilli," "Ode: Anus," and "What magic is"; *Her Words:* "The maidens of spring" and "Night sweat"; *A Literary Field Guide to Southern Appalachia:* "Mountain brook lamprey"; *Marks of the Witch:* (chapbook) "What time it is" and "Witch hairs"; *New Ohio Review:* "Happy lamp"; *North American Review:* "Butterflies, Urine" and "Ode: Yeast"; *North Carolina Literary Review:* "Campus, August evening, plague year," "Cursive," "The narrative of stones," and "When you know a witch's true name"; *Plant-Human Quarterly:* "Willow Minnows" and "Spring Tonic"; *Poetry South:* "The color of aquamarine: a spell for blessing" and "What magic is"; *RHINO:* "Ode: Anus"; *Southern Humanities Review:* "Lactobacilli"; *storySouth:* "Black wool coat on a hook"; *WNC Magazine:* "Choptank bluegills take part in the creation of the world"; *Women Speak* anthology, the Women of Appalachia Project: "During the long meeting things begin to change," "Earthflash," "Four goldenrods," "The haunting," "Spring tonic," "This house," and "Until the cows come home."

Grounding

What magic is

> *I opened a door.*
> —RAHUL DUBEY[1]

Not the knife to the throat
of cat or goat: that's making
something else sacrifice
what you have to give
yourself. Not the iron-
racked will behind LaLaurie's
attic room.[2] Not praying,
while waving a wand, "Let someone
burn, but not me, not me."
Magic's not safety
where there's none, it's not
what gets called magic.

Nor, either, the transfiguration
of cabbage through
fermentation, meat
through heat, Maillard
reaction, light
through photosynthesis,
because that's something
else, that's miracle. Magic's
the human thing,
the one right word, deed, touch,
at the one right time.

---

1. During protests of the murder of George Floyd, Rahul Dubey opened the door of his Washington, DC, townhouse on June 1, 2020, to give shelter to about sixty protestors who were being pepper-sprayed by police while fleeing.

2. Marie Delphine LaLaurie was a serial murderer and torturer of people who were enslaved in her New Orleans household in the 1830s.

The power of the words
God bless, or *I was
wrong.* Of Black Elk's
rain cloud. Of one
man opening
a door to one small
apartment to admit
sixty weeping people
fleeing faceless shields.
Of pouring water and milk
over their burning eyes.

Witches' correspondences :: it's complicated

East the air: hour of equinox
dawn through brown smog
of woodstove car exhaust smokestack
factories across the border in Tennessee
hour and season of the wind
with its scent of wet earth   its reek
of papermill   hour of the mind
clouded with doubt   hour of the words
and the diminishing birds   the towhee
beginning to call first light into invasive
cruciform bittercress glittering with dew
into the purring chime of the redphase
screechowl in the smoky dawn's pearlhaze:

that's morning, that's east,
but each day you wade in deeper:
particles entangling until no single one
can be described or even seen
separate from others   until to look
at one is to look at another   across oceans
across lightyears   across oaks' communion
through sticky white fungal threads
which knit together the whole world
through ecosystems imbricated
in one another and in the coal ash
spill   the kudzu swell   the cancerlung
of rainforest the human
and the not   everything everywhere
        we are here
        are here
        are here
everything you never
planned   which pried you
open as a root splits a rock
everything fusing into right-here's burningpoint:

the afternoon-south of this one life
the flow-focus shattered again and again
the struggling will toward change   the desire
and its fulfillment or not   the tumbleweed flashing
into fire as it rolls over droughtparched
continents, a wheel of flame   before which whole
coasts incinerate like witches   and this one day:
one last almost-gone puma outstretched
in the August sun westering through Lammastide's
oven to pause in its own blaze
to bake the seeds of the nodding grasses   to crackle
the crust and raise crumb in the hot new bread
hoop of fire in which the god
with his three eyes and four arms dances
the world into and out of creation
made   unmade   remade again

before slipping into the flickering spiral
of the yellow walnut leaf falling
downward   westward   back toward visions
seen through water   back to the heaving depths
where menhaden spring before needle-
filled bluefish jaws   to the unending gyres
of plastic particles   microbeads neoprene
bottles   tiny caps   Styrofoam cups
and grocery bags grocery bags grocery bags
masquerading as jellyfish
back to droplets rising   rising up into cold rain
filling the wells of earth as it comes
walking   sweeping its soiled silver
veil across the western sea

And north at last the earth   the body
flesh of the earth: the mud
and the blood   the bones
and the stones   the bears the raccoons
midnight of the long night
bottom of the long spin
of the year   of the spokes
of that year's doublespiral
wheel merging and twining
into the biological molecule combining
and recombining   changing
and bearing the nanoplastic seeds
of its own unravel   its fraying
strands inscribed with the blueprints
of life   with the world
with the word   with the everchanging
slowly shattering   and more slowly rewritten
Word

Why I'm here

The mama and daddy who never split, or hit
each other, or died leaving me to the wrong
relative. The bad daycare I never had to survive,
the bad grades I sometimes deserved but didn't get:
everyone already knew I must be clever.
The arrest that didn't come when I came to school
with a pocketful of dry bayberry leaves
that looked so much like weed:
I was timid and white and wore ivy
sweaters. That night not spent in lockup,
those months not beaten up in juvie. Everything
I never smoked or shot up or stole or wanted to;
my life was that clear, that good. And got better.
The tuition I didn't pay, because of the waiver.
The abortions I never had, thanks to the condoms
I could afford. These fingers heavy
machinery didn't sever, in the factory job
I never had to take and be grateful. The bullet
my brother never met, the war I never served. What
privilege looks like: everything that never.

Witch hairs

Not hairs. Boar
bristles, thistle
thorns, catfish barbels,
wolf whiskers, sprung
from a nose and chin
that've called to each
other forty-five years
across the short chasm
of philtrum and lips, and only
now draw nearer
and nearer, connected
by folds turned to grooves
turned to dry ditches
only deepened by the rare
brackish flash flood.
Old women have always been
witches, and these are
the marks of the witch:
these wires with roots
deeper than teeth.
They smack of a witch-curse,
a desperate bargain,
the kind of deal
you strike with the dark
when there's little
left in your hand—
two low hearts,
a single waiting spade—
a deal with the powers of air
and hair.

In the hour of fire

Feeling the shiver of fire, the flesh-
crawl of the coming flash,
you tear at covers, fling limbs wide,
raise back off bed to dissipate
the roaring flame-wave
thinking as always of the burning
of witches without what was called *mercy
of strangulation*, though the nave
of the body is not so much kinder,
especially to women. Here it comes,
suffocating heat, breathless flush.
Pores evert, gasp pinpricks of sweat,
and if you will, you can choose air
conditioning, close windows, close
out summer: industrial
magic, if you're willing to burn
the earth to save yourself, if you can choose
how many writhing and waking nights
justify one more increment of heat to broil
alive a world in its own hour of fire.
If you can choose yourself over everyone
and everything else, as most of us
will. And you will.
If not tonight, then tomorrow
night. In fear of wildfire,
landslide, whirlwind, flood,
great powers loosed, in fear
of what this flesh can suffer.
When the witchfinders hurt us enough,
we'll say anything, accuse anyone. We will
walk into the hall, raise our hands
in the ritual gesture, touch the snowflake
rune, we will choose the air.

The broom closet

Deeper in it than most brooms, you hang out with the mops
and the rags, breathing up irony and Pledge:
your worship is beautiful and sacred, and you must never tell.
They may not burn you alive now, but who's not afraid
of fire, noose, abuse, who's not afraid
even of contempt, credibility torched, windy slurs whistled
incessant as mockingbird trills? But the thing with closets:
at some point the dustpans have nothing new to say,
while out there quivers the living world you claim
to hold sacred, wood thrushes fluting true
before three measures of silence like notes
in another register, pond-toads you'd never lick
or stew, shape-shifted from their silky-black gold-
dusted water-slime into soft-dappled new.
And the thing with brooms: ride them or not,
their use is to clean rooms, exercise
the domestic arts, exorcise despair. So let
the wind bang open your door like a bell,
watch the threshold unfold both ways, an opened book,
see the sun's three octillion blazing candles
always already answering your prayer
for light: at some point, the right broom drives
decades of dust out the door before you. It turns
those stifling puffs to sparkling spiral galaxies on the air
where the mockingbirds' wing-blooms spin like pinwheels.

When you know a witch's true name

she has to do what you ask. If she tries
to refuse, her name lets you tighten the wire
on marrow-fears she's spent forever
trying to hide, secret shames which sicken
her so she'd almost rather strangle than share:
the reason she wraps herself in that caul
of hexes, chainsaws, shielding spells.
This makes witches cautious.
Except something in them, in us
all, wants to hear someone say
our names with recognition, no matter
what comes after. Curled round
our glint of treasure, our shimmer
of power, we're gongs hung
to tremble to our one true name
or one true question, the one we've awaited
forever, whose answer is our whole lives,
the one almost no one is interested
enough to ask. It's why I'd come
if you summoned me up, despite.
If you knew the right question,
I would tell you anything.

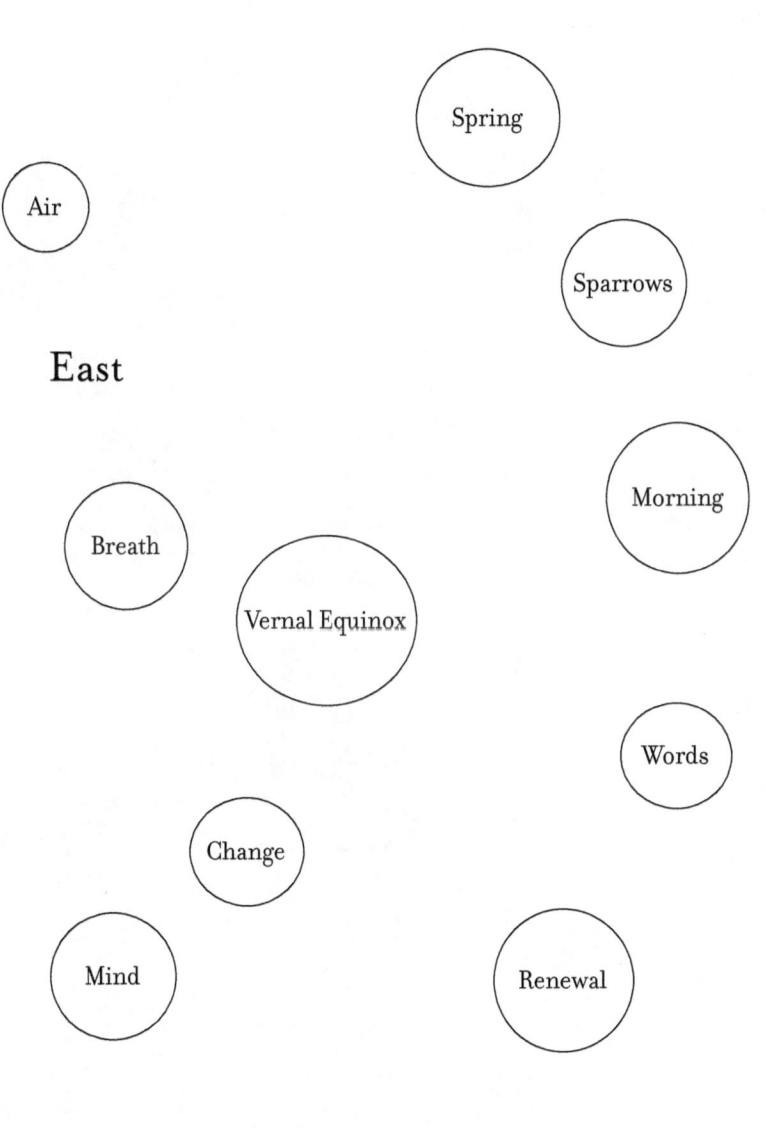

Butterflies, urine

> *It did not occur to him that [the fates] might be engaged in*
> *casting dice against gravity; that mice and men, soil and songs,*
> *might be merely ways to retard the march of atoms to the sea.*
> —ALDO LEOPOLD, "Odyssey," *A Sand County Almanac*

Over knobby shallows, through long femoral marrows
the narrow red rivers run, sluicing to the kidneys'
thinner creeks the foundations of life in this world,
calcium and magnesium dissolved from bonemelt
as human height slides away, sucked back by blood
heeding earthpull. Nitrogen to feed soil. Sodium salts,
loved and craved. All life the scramble
for minerals, and none of them yours for long,
as you remember when you crouch, under April
sun striking mica-shine from bare limbs, to return
borrowed water to the papery leaf-floor, and the air
around you ignites into breathing and beating
wings. Periwinkle flecks and flakes unfurling
long spiral tongues to your sparkling stream, tiger
swallowtails quivering striped vanes over muddy
patches of piss, pollen-edged mourning cloaks
mourning nothing so hard that they can't slip
in for a sip of you—vivid ephemerals
oblivious to whatever you need
them to represent, drawn in frantic flitter
to the patter of water for what they need,
invisible particles of bone, of salt,
to slake their thirst, so like your own.

Can, worms

This time say it. Open your mouth and open that can,
though pause first to suck breath at the welling slice
as ragged lid slides windward over thumb:
despite steel-stitched seamless near-eternal
embalming of fifteen perfect ounces, never
trust a can, rust and rupture claim them all
in the end, and while you gout crimson over light-switch
and ceiling, here come the worms, welling too
from their can, writhing together in what might be love
—hermaphroditic, of course, each worm
twining around its equal and likeness,
each swelling clitellum packed with both-and—
or combat to the glistening mucosal
death: with worms it's hard to tell
unless you're a worm. Slender pink S-curves,
whipworms, slow-pulsing segments of tape,
nematodes, umber-red nightcrawlers distended
as if with venom, knotting and clenching and slipping
through knots of themselves like hagfish, like Houdini
escaping three anchor chains six padlocks
and an executioner's hood, from a tank bulging
with water, or worms, blood smearing everywhere
while worms keep slithering and bubbling
up from where they've been entombed
too long, pressed airlessly together where they'll never
fit again. It's too late now, so say it.
Tip up that can and tumble loose
a loveknot of pink and gray, twining
your fingers like kinked coils of telephone
cord, these words, I mean these worms,
that you've clamped back since the days
when telephones had cords. Turn
that dirty steel wheel on your own gripped lips,
say it now, and go on saying it as these worms

ramp and hump toward deep waves of open earth,
shivering an ecstasy of helminthoid release. And you there,
standing in the chaos, streaked and sullied
with blood and ichor: now you can drop that ruined
cage you still clutch. They're free now, they're out
of your grasp, crawling their way through the world
into which they will burrow and till and snout.
The world where they will change everything.

The haunting

It all happened here.
Maybe they should've stayed
where there was sun morning
and noon, where the scarred stairs smelled
so warmly of dog, but that place was small;
this one was new, its stairs varnished
slick and clear. Here the dogs
had to be put down: first the blind
pug, then the tall mutt. Then
things got worse. A spouse
on the couch sent the spouse
at the other end messages brimming
with acid. At the Superbowl
party, the onion dip tasted of tears.
There were the secret cell
phone, the hidden credit card,
the frozen accounts, the plague
of lies. The AC grew colder,
then glacial. Kids slipped on the steps;
the floors, tasting blood, grew sharp.
Paintings tipped on the walls,
edging toward doors
which kept whispering shut.
A stove handle pulled half away
and stayed there hanging.
The washer clawed holes in a blouse.
Though no necks broke
on the stairs, it was enough,
the house now wakened by pain
into its own nightmare life.
The great oak began bleeding
black, leaning out of the ground,
and as it fell the dirt shuddered
and groaned. Lost in the altered

dimensions, the twisting
halls which led to unsuspected cells
where no rooms had been, those within
looked at one another and spoke
the words there was no unsaying,
from which there was no way home.

Dupont Circle, skunk

When the waft of stink eddied on Q
where it spills into Connecticut, one opal
evening in the last of March,
it meant the change was here.
Its reek broke the stride of walkers
with bulging bags; a courier's blue
Schwinn shuddered and sprang away. Next year
no one would remember this,
the voice of the turtle
dove, the terrible passion
of Pepé Le Pew, the love note
of the silent striped weasel. *Are you there?*
it called, courting the clouds
and the crescent moon. *are you my kind?*
do you know my name?
Never! choked the woman in fur.
Nunh-unh! the taximan grunted.
But the eleven-year-old on the skateboard,
rolling over bumpy concrete toward lights
and supper, that girl paused, lifted her head, nose
flared for what smelled so rank,
so strong, green and new as a swamp
cabbage, so out there on the rim
between winter afternoon and spring
night, and though she'd never met this scent
in all her brief life, she whispered *yes:*
I remember, maybe, I know you,
yes, from some time before,—
and with the word, April
happened, April unfurled
its invisible pollen, its pheromonal magic,
over the concrete, over the skateboard,
over Q Street where it flows
into Connecticut Avenue.

Willow minnows

At the bottom of the mill's tethered water
wheel the willows shed slender pale-yellow
leaves into the millrace, slow now and low
in late September; you stand waiting
for their drift to grow heavy as they take
up the brown water, but you are not ready
when the leaves all at once become shiners, minnows,
begin to swim on their own, faster than the stream
or the season, darting and glinting in a sudden
sparkling shoal, flicking away downstream
right through December's glass icicles and
February's freezing mud into April, where they spring
up from the tailrace and back onto the bare
whippy limbs, golden as the young sun
and deepening as you watch into thin viridian,
so that the willows now blooming their powdery caterpillar
catkins arch and stretch out new fingerling
leaves of air-breathing light-drinking photosynthesizing fish.

The neighborhoods of housewives

The hurrying clouds, after rain,
are washed white as sheets, undersides
alone shadowed with deep gray-blue.
Ganomai's doing washing too,
rinsing a month of shed skinflakes
from scarlet quilt-covers, pinning
them high to fill with the great wind.
Some neighborhoods are cul-de-sacs
of mud or concrete, some dusty
dirt roads with houses set far back,
marked only by a stark mailbox:
but all across the world's full curves,
these streets are theirs by midmorning,
queendoms of invisible work
that goes unpaid. Storm-broken sticks
gleam on wet roads; at the wood-verge
at a street's end, a wind-shaken
pond flashes and shines, and lotus
buds, where Sita lets a fretting
child drag her by the hand. Aje,
meanwhile, counting cowries, budgets
for market bills. Irene brokers
tense peace between two squalling sons;
Sibyl begins the eternal
ritual of making order,
picking up, sorting endless toys
and clothes and towels, foreseeing
which ones will first be shouted for.
Bridget kneels down before a stove,
feeding it splinters of dry grass
and breathing up the choking smoke,
while, crouching in her furrowed yard,
Kianda reknots the old net
that lets her children bring home fish.

This morning every neighborhood
is all their own, and though they work
without ceasing at creation
and maintenance, they also pause
a short moment to raise their heads
and let the sun illuminate
their scoured faces with its old light
until they shine like goddesses.

Spring tonic

Every year there's watercress in the runoff
ditch, froth of foam-bloom in the culvert that drains
a highway a parking lot a construction
site a few gratuitous cow
fields, meaning there's not enough iodine
in the world, that cress will never be safe
to eat. So with field-mustard creasies
not up yet, you turn for your equinox green
back to muddy yards, cracks in foundations
of buildings, hairy bittercress:
its tiny pepper-spice, its blunt scallop-curl
leaves, its satyr-labor to spread its glitter
of cruciform flowers over gardens waste
places intramural fields by detonating slender
siliques in a micro-ballista sputter
of seed. Chopped into salad, sipped
over soup, gnawed in the raw, it's what you need
now: deep vivid bite of what
comes first, blazes its way, takes
cold rain-slits into its own
flesh, takes the first and only chance
it has. Spring tonic that wrings
mouth and bowels because still fresh
from the dark cauldron's boil and spit;
taste of renewal strong enough, in its spiral
basal-rosette heart, for this very world:
its sudsy ditches greasy roads whirling weed
eaters grinding clocks night sticks raised
to strike. Taste of resistance photo-
synthesized into unfettered
exuberance. Attar of bitter.

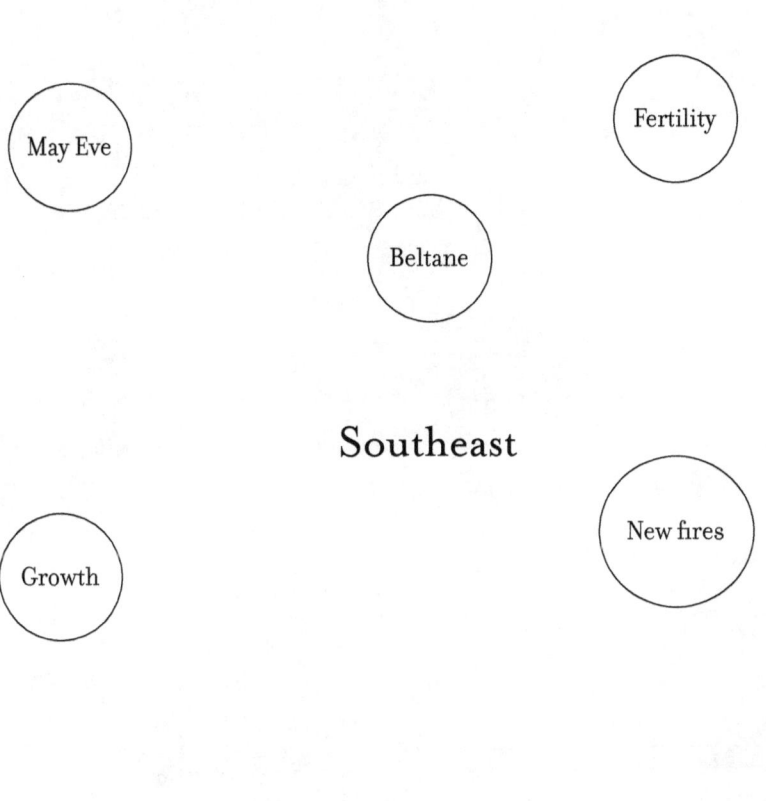

Lactobacilli

Invisible and everywhere,
on your hands,
on your shoes,
in your nose, lining
your ells of bowel,
we lay down scraps
of chromosomes
and pick them up
like screwdrivers
or cards, if half the cards
are wild as sauerkraut—
e. coli, listeria,
seaweed, straight flush.

Nor are you you,
some single entity
cruising the lonely black
star-seas like a whale:
you are a ship, a host,
the poker table.
We are crew
and players and spirit,
your spirit, the one many-
bodied soul you can know
for sure. *Genius loci*.
Spirits of place.
Full house.

This house

The year's sauerkraut is coldly cooking
itself down in the cellar of the house
whose concrete floor keeps the bodies down.

Upstairs, dogs are fighting
or play-fighting on the skin rug near the stove
where birch-twigs turn back to their native flame
and a man is kneading bread like living flesh.

Some of the children play Balderdash
while the rest watch TV, all
but the two who are tormenting a third
into pitching herself down the stairs:
another emergency call.

This house has sealed rooms,
more than I'll ever see.
Some are full of stones; at the turn
of the weather, smell the chill of their breath.
Listen: the cry of a door's secret hinge.

Outside, there are more windows than inside,
flashing sunrise before fading
into siding as the bright day swells.

The whitefoot mice know. When they slip out
of the walls into the rooms we see,
we find them next day on the rug
in a soil of blood: the cats also know.

Some rooms are roofed with limbs
interlaced, floored with a rubble
of roots. Some rooms are packed tight
with rotting shirts, spoiled meat.

That whisper of water isn't the pipes
but the creek that runs under the floor.

The attic's flying squirrels give birth to kits.
There's a dead bumblebee on a sill.
Sunchokes ripen toward December,
the roasting, the eating.

The washing is never done, the mail
heaps up, the children
keep torturing each other
as soon as you turn away.
From the day you sign the lease, you're behind.

In the eaves, the wren sings all year.
Under the foundation, the dead do, too.

Nothing is ever finished, nothing
ever simple, the number
of the rooms will never be known,
not here, not in this house.

The stars of love

We were the stars of love, then of marriage:
Sonny and Cher, White Stripes, Fleetwood
Mac, you were my Air Supply and we
could make all the stadiums rock five
times a week or twice a day, could laugh
in bad weeks that we'd fallen all the way
to the national average, our fights brief
and curt before we loved again
even harder, each the other's number one
fan, any potential breakup no more likely
than a black hole threatening to break up with the star
next door that it's busy deep-throating right
into the next dimension. Through our thirties,
our forties, our blaze of solar radiance warmed every
planet, flared from every moon, made
every speck of space-dust shine till it cast
its own line of shadow two parsecs long.
Other than everyone else who'd ever been down
this street in their own white limousines, who knew
that we'd become first red giants, then white dwarfs,
then Jefferson Starship, then Air Supply 2020? Or that,
as our endless fusion factory finally began to cool,
the invisible gravity wells dragging us back together
and back together would flare upward, outward,
until now we cling still closer in the cold black bed
of the void, drawn into ever-tighter orbit
by some greater mystery, some dark matter deeper
and more tender than hydrogen's burn; that, original fires
sinking, we'd become binary for true, companion
stars whose burnt cores swing around one
another through the endless eons between here
and heat death, making their love out of helium,
carbon, oxygen, out of nothing at all.

Artemis in Appalachia

Al and Acton found her, the woman with thirteen breasts
lapped over chest and belly, smooth curves like stones
or egg-corns. They were lighting for deer,
bow season, sinking crescent, clear evening after late thunder;
she lay curled on burnt earth in a stand of black willow
and bald cypress down-creek, air reeking ozone,
and from the flash of their lamps they saw the return
flash of deer-eyes, heard the brush rustle with rabbits,
before they all faded back, left only a phoebe bobbing its tail.
Acton wanted to try if he couldn't fetch back one
of those deer, but Al said what's wrong with you, come on,
Act, look here. When he touched her shoulder, she spoke
in tongues or something, dazed, didn't seem to know
her own name. They walked her to the pickup
and bumped and jounced back to town,
trying not to stare at all those tits, Acton
still muttering about the deer. Another time
they would've thought hospital, but they didn't know
what to make of her, lightning and breasts and all,
so they headed for Otis's place. Otis had been a Marine
medic, and he'd trained in Atlanta for the law
and travelled some, he'd know what to do,
and what Otis said was, boys, it's not right.
One breast can send a man baying like a dog
through the trees to savage some other man;
even the Greek lady on the courthouse covers them up,
and she's just got two. It's too much, it's fearful,
somehow. Otis's old hound Blue, the one he hadn't the heart
to shoot though he couldn't run much anymore,
dropped his chin on her knee, so they left her there on the rug
by Blue and dug through the drawer where a girl or two
had left a few things over the years, and came up
with a skirt and three bras, not much
but worth a try. And they tried. Tried the hooks

in the back, then in the front. Tugged the elastic straps
down to the band of the skirt. She still seemed moonstruck,
just let them work. Al held the flowered blue one stretched
as far as he could while Acton stuffed two breasts
into one cup, thinking he was getting somewhere
till the first one poured right out the other side
and Al took a hook under his thumbnail like a bamboo
sliver and Otis got popped hard in the lip
when the underwire split. At last they corralled
eight of those things into three bras, by then they were all
sweating, but the lower row was still out there
in front of God and everybody when Blue
raised his speckled head and put up a cry that struck them dumb
and shivered the hair on their necks. While they stared
like deer in headlights, every dog in town, it sounded like,
broke into terrible song, *awaaaoohhh, awaaaoh, no, no, no,*
and that lightningstruck woman with the thirteen breasts
drew a big breath like she'd fallen into wellwater
as every bra on every breast burst and rang
like a big spring snapping back. She snatched
up Act's compound bow where he'd dropped it on the couch
and ran past them straight out the door, and Blue
went bounding behind, howling like the end of the world.
They took after her, Otis hollering for Blue
and Acton yelling that that bow had cost him
three-nineteen-ninety-nine and Al getting his foot
all snarled in the black bra trimmed with gold lace
before he could catch up. They never saw a sign
of her, and Act never did get back his bow,
but in the cold dawn Blue came limping back, red-eyed
and muddy and stiff with beggar ticks. And that's the story
as I heard it told, except Acton and Al got a deer
each before the moon came full again.

Those boys did the best they knew,
and if it didn't end just right, it might've been
a whole lot worse if they'd done any different:
so whether it's tits or it's deer, you watch yourself.
Even the dogs know there's more out there
than we ever see, and thirteen's just plain too many.

Earth says

I am your mother as the horse
is mother to the louse, endlessly
intricate interlocking systems
which the blissfully sucking louse
cannot imagine and never must,
which it sums up
in some louse-sign for God
a quiver of hairs of the thorax,
a shimmer of inarticulate
gratitude for satiation and for
preservation of self, self, self.
I am sick of it, mother
with eight billion toddlers
not counting my beautiful beetles,
a horse plagued with lice, and yet.
I am your mother as you are mother
to the mosquito which hovers
over your arm as you write,
mote of thirsty gold quivering
with desperation to the boom
of great rivers in blue tunnels
and pipes just below the soft leather
scrim of skin, endless life
you'll never miss and won't let her have,
enough for a thousand generations.
If she tries to drink you will want
to swat her flat, and she must try,
for her unborn young, for her life. And maybe
eventually, weary of swatting,
worn down by importunity,
unwilling compassion, fear
of the insect apocalypse blossoming
all around you like a mushroom
cloud, you will incline your head. Fall

still. Let her drink her fill
and float away, a dandelion spore
on the summer air, in the hot flash
of May morning light.

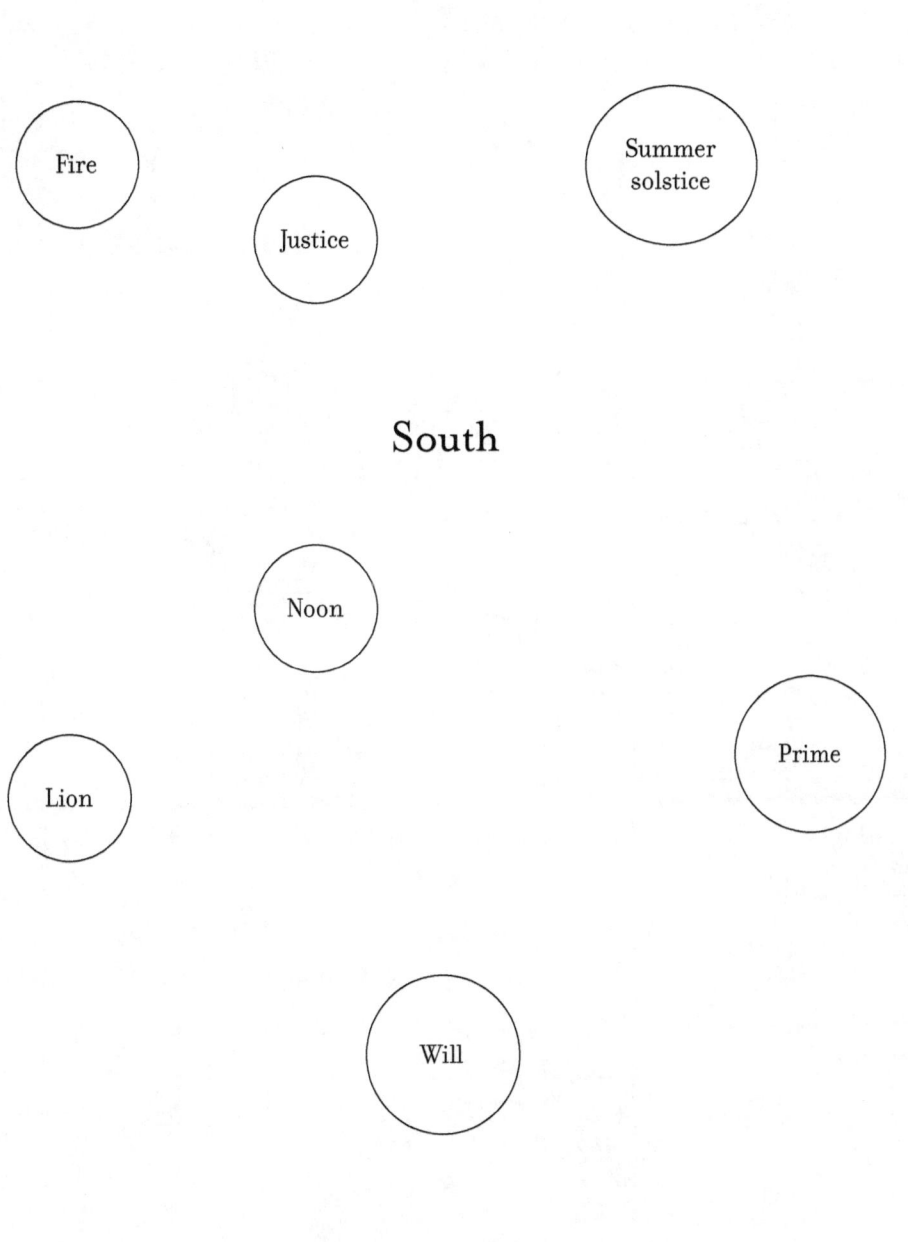

When you tell me I'm being racist

> *Therefore if thine enemy hunger, feed him; if he thirst, give him drink:*
> *for in so doing thou shalt heap coals of fire on his head.*
> —ROMANS 12:20, KJV

When you tell me I'm being racist,
it's a strange gift. Dangerous.
Eerie, too, as you pry at your chest,
scoop aside hard white
ribs, dark blood, and offer
what you wrench free—a hot cinder
split, riven, glazed gloss-black
though at the draft's touch a flash
flushes through it, glows
clear vermillion then sinks back
to its wary smolder, burn
you've borne forever
but which I'm afraid to take
in my bare hand, ashamed
not to: fire which can wake
cold votives into yellow stars
in a house without power, kindle
a stove into warmth to cook
coffee or chili or cornbread,
flare into flame to light
a whole world, light
by which I must see you
anew, and this world, also
myself, knowing it's going to hurt.
You can't trust me to see
the gift's grace, receive
let alone embrace the burning
wafer. Yet you still stand,
chest-cleft folding slowly together

as we wait to see whether
I will, as you go on holding
out your lifted palm, coal pulsing
redder, skin beginning to smoke.

Nail garden

Ranks of women crouch at feet of pale
giantesses, breathing up acetone
formaldehyde miscarriage cancer
in clear cauls. Everything damp, shriveled
fingertips, prickly calves, women who
paint clawed feet with flame-flower, topaz
sparkles, slate-silver of ocean lost
behind thousand-mile crabgrass and strip
malls, who gouge dirt of this world from horn-
plates and skin creases, chiming to one
another in registers unheard
by giantesses, songs from a gone home.
Freckled giantess slips off Naots,
says she only wants her heel-callous
filed if it doesn't cost extra; woman
kneeling before her nods in answer,
woman who had studied medicine
back before she fled the coup for these
rows of wet feet, this garden of nails,
woman who had specialized in cancer.

Ode: Candlefat

Grass shaping sunlight
into sugar, cows converting
grass to white tallow,
honey-fed bees secreting
dander that turns to amber
wax, avocados' lush
yellow-green butter, sediment-
pressed prehistoric bacterial
mats torched and flickering blue
across the steel-silver grid: fat.
How living things trap energy,
capture light. The candlefat
a large human hauls in his back,
her breasts, his deep navel
curve or her rumpled buttocks,
could dazzle alleys
or caverns with sunfire
he can never set
down, starflare she bears
and burns, which is why
the thin yearn to burn
the fat at the stake:
they know how the heavy
are also the most light, light
incarnate, sun made flesh,
pulsing candent batteries stretched tight
with light sealed and stored cell
by cell by cell, shining
picosecond hearthfires flicking up
and flaring out in all that crackling ice-
black night, long
illuminations of the longer

dark in the steady flame-
radiance of their bodies,
themselves, their wild
extravagance of candlelight.

In the plague year, I remember pinkeye

Then, plague stalked where I turned
my demon gaze, drawn
by basilisk glare, two hexes sunk
in pink pits, crimson-
rimmed, rabbit-rosy, blood-
blurred: a stroll through a store
could infect a town. One blink
and you too would waken
with eyes gum-glued together, perfect
tiny sphere of bright mucus
beading each lash. I tried
not to look, hid with shades
down, worked to block
the awful gift, dreading
spreading harm, wreaking wrong, loosing
purulent yellow ooze
upon a cowering world
with the cursed vision, evil evil eye.
But now putrescence comes
through the breath:
each exhaled unseen viral micro-
bubble a malediction
of pestilence and scourge. And
almost worse, the curse
is on, and in, the words,
each one having become
incantation of bane, trapped,
at best, in mask. It has taken
months to say even this, each
sweet word laden and freighted
with death, and all they used
to mean, irrelevant. Thank you.

Perdóname. I love you. I wish
you'd stop talking. Have
some seitan marsala. A blessing
on your house in this ravaged
year. Hallelujah. *Inshallah.*

Night sweat

Needleprick droplets, snake-smooth,
ripe as cataracts or pearl-berries
of poison ivy, seep
up lucid puddles and pools
of sweat between breasts,
into the folds of sheets and knees,
into the collarbone-hollow,
sullen-bubbling steam-wreathed
hot springs into which you can sink—
mere-monster retreating to her lair,
witch dunked in a sun-hot pond—
down into the magma-warmed
underworld which flushes the skin
above to rose-mallow, swells
arteries with surging flashfloods
of blood, making of pores deep-sea
volcanic vents where tardigrades
turn and trundle through pools of you
as you drop past them into the well
of this body, the hotspring of all
you know as self: and no
knowing yet if this is the first
baptism or the last—
if you'll die in your youthful
innocence, limp sack of skin
dragged out to the pious
mutter of prayers for the scalded-
alive, the lost, the drowned,
or if you'll live, reborn
from the cauldron like some soggy phoenix
to be shunned and stoned as the hag
you can't help but become,
different and strange as cooked
flesh is from raw,
transmuted, appalling, irretrievably changed.

Earthflash

Some night when this shriveling flesh's cup
of sudden fire splashes itself too high,
I'll thrash off the smothering choke of down,
pincer-plucked from some long-slaughtered goose,
and, half-sleepwalking, pad into the black
and white where the yard spreads beneath the moon
to press myself to cool and gritty dirt,
splay out in an X to return this witch-
burning volcanic sear to the restless
flow of magma heaving far below.
Then will I feel the suffocating scald
dissipate into grainy-cold white sand,
black humus, rust-stained clay? or will a mist
of warmth flush back up, from an earth itself
a witch feeling the terror rise like heat
from the licking, whispering wood that's heaped
at her bound feet, earth itself a woman
in the net of her own sweat, walking out
into her bitter black expanse to arch
against the void in futile pangs to ease
what's cooking her alive? over, over,
pressing her round back and her round belly
to the cold, a woman pelt-plagued by scourge
of fleas or ticks who never cease biting
and sucking, injecting her with buboes
and Lyme and with the smoky red-brown haze
of hot flashes in which she rolls and rolls
and rolls, while here upon her skin, we burn.

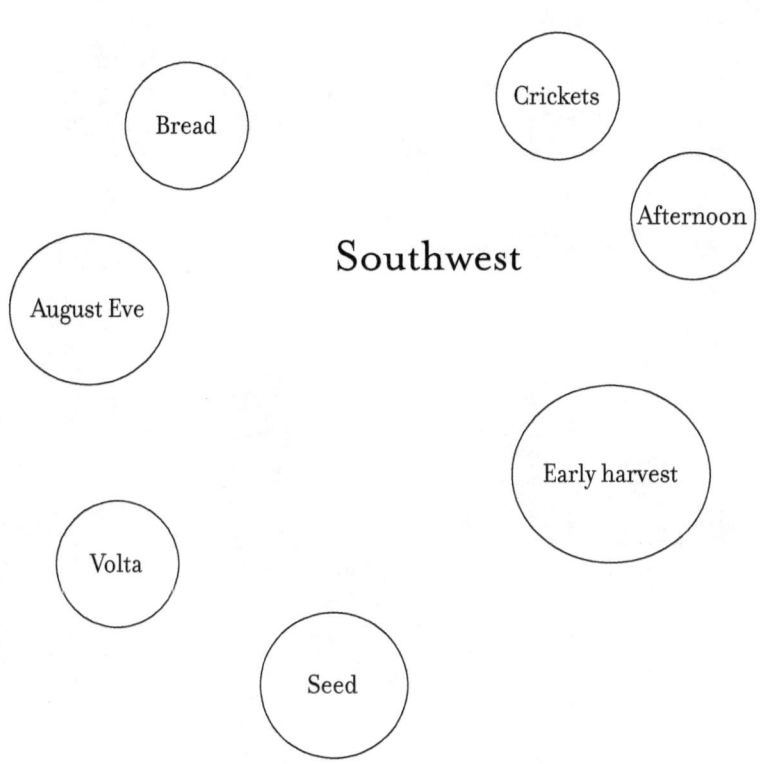

What time it is

By the sun, it's the time of the dying
god, the burngold buckwheat scattering
to the furrow to rise again (all save
the altered terminator grains).
By the world's moon, it's wax-
time, swelling gibbous, every night
kinder to the uncanny
coyote, the plundering skunk.
By the wombmoon it's the time
of the dark and the reaper, black
blood poised to flood
forth in a rusty algae-bloom, though
for now stubbornly clutching
those curved walls like clots
of bats in the caves of afternoon.
By this moon women kill and are glad.
By this life it's high summer, prime
of fire, no eclipse forecast
today. By the school it's New Year's,
new pencils, smooth paper rolling
up from flattened forests, and
by the Mayan temples, any second now
the end of the world will descend
All the clocks quarrel: zero,
one, tock, tock, tock,
pull down, restore, rein
and spur. No one knows what time it is—
apogee, perigee; Advent or Lent—
and every moment a new year commences,
we walk through, into the next
year, the fresh blood-beaded
second, through those broad-beamed doors.

Campus, August evening, plague year

Cloudy skies, twilight, student voices rising
around the fountain, kids probably not masked
against contagion; but I don't go
check, I'm afraid to know. Twenty-one
years I've made this short
walk after teaching evening
classes: past the bell tower,
which twenty-one years ago shimmered
with the invisible orbits of nighthawks
and bats, before the insect
crash. Past yellow lights coming
on in windows as if by magic;
exactly by magic. Further back,
a decade before
those twenty-one years,
four years of nights when
my own dorm shone
like that, reflected in its wavering
pond like a riverboat. Here,
no pond, though the lit dorms still
glow like vast boats, alive now
with survivors, borne
along on the unceasing irresistible
streams of youth and the young
pouring into this place and out again,
making and changing their gritty beds: forever
the same, unquenchably new,
                    except this year,
when we old ones hold grim pools
betting how long the young will be allowed
to stay. How long before the gatherings
are shattered by plague, beds stripped,
fountains run dry. How many
will sicken, or worse. Where they'll go,

those for whom this was their only
safe place, and those who were on the edge
already, what bones they'll shatter
when they're pushed off. Whether any
will ever have their few years
out of time, drift-anchored on the running
stream, all I was given that I can't
give them. And below the waterlines
of the big lifeboats now,
how much green seep wells in, how fast.
No bet, I say aloud, hurrying
faster. I'm ashamed to know.

The maidens of spring

Your skirts grow downward.
Sun calls for a straw fedora, black band, silk roses,
long after live roses have all gone to hip
and thorn. For decades you were the maiden
of spring, years before death and his black chariot:
sleeveless years, bright-skinned, years of breasts
which had no brief with gravity,
there you were. Then you weren't.
Now the maidens of spring live
over in Narcissus Court, calling and chattering
like young starlings, *sparkling
stars, crop tops, April evening, new,
new!* and here you are, wrapped in a caul
of soft fat that won't pry loose, adorned
like a catfish with trailing whiskers
at breast and groin and chin.
To be the maiden again, you'll have to die,
and you're not ready. There's life in you yet,
wrinkled but sweet as a Gala.
You sag closer to earth, and gravity
doesn't let go. It's August, a new
millennium, and the years roll only
one way. Yet here
you still are, in the long blue dress
with sleeves, in the blue shadow
of your hat, the woman of summer,
crowned with roses.

During the long meeting things begin to change:

scowl lines and smile lines slowly become grooves,
then gullies into which wild horses could wander
like canyon mazes and die there, unable to find
water or the way out, and the oblong yellow notepad
on the conference table reveals itself to be a trap-
door with an iron ring, the kind laid in old houses'
kitchen floors. It lifts into one stealthy hand
with a quiet hinge-cry; you step
softly to the seat of your chair and then
to the tabletop and then down the unpainted,
unrailed plank stairs into the cool
smells of dog hair, stone and the soundless
water that seeps from stone. The light, a faint
gray gleam from a dusty ground-pane,
glints briefly in canning jars filmed with grime.
Startled by shift and creak, a brown wolf
spider, palm-broad, pauses for an eight-eyed
stare, then flicks away at the renewed voice-
rumble overhead. In the twilight you can see
the foundations, the underpinnings
of everything: the pillars bearing up the ceiling-
joists were once small trees, cut trunks sanded
something like smooth, harder now than cement,
shielded from weather and rot. A hundred years
and more, they have held up what's overhead,
and now, steady and firm, they hold
even more: the budget on the table, the hissing
heating ducts, the freight and weight
of administrative hierarchy, the oblivious
committee setting deadlines, earnestly debating dates
while, underground, you stoop to the lime-
washed floor to take up a round gold
rutabaga, still unshriveled, which someone before
you must have left or forgotten here: a token
of faith or warning, a word in code, a sign.

When you stop by High Noon for a new pierce

first Jordyn measures   then the deep
              hard helix pinch punches
                          cartilage apart to receive
                                      the two-millimeter dangle
                                                of silver crescent moon
the spangle of movement   the moment
        of glint.   Because today
                the parents are still well
            enough to ask later   *why but why*
    would you want to?   Because today
you can walk and cycle and paddle
            a kayak named after a shark   Because

today   alive in a life
            not even a millisecond long for a shale slice
                or the garnet grit of shore-sand
                      let alone a moon
      you have and you are
           a body   opening
            its needle-sized wound
                  to frivolity adornment celebration
Because

        the noon wind fills the leaves' bright sails   Because tonight
      all night   you will feel   inside the curve
            of your shell-whorled ear
                tugging at the tides and the tilt
                      of earth's axis   turning
      one face always toward you   one always away
  the tiny moon
shine and chime

Fuck: A blessing

When we say *fuck you*, why isn't it blessing,
this wish for you to know glorious release with another
of your kind, and, after, that weightless drift
through the pool of peace at the base of your spine?
What's accursed in being breathlessly desired
just as you are, your bulges and flushes and knees,
your tantrums at the DMV? *Fuck you* should mean
let the wind be ever, may the odds be ever,
Namaste, have a blessed, may you rock on your joy
like the paper nautilus on its native wave, hover
and shimmer at the brink of the high cliff
before your dissolution into sunlight.

And so it could be, except grammar. Except
transitive verbs. Except English, where *fuck*
is like *colonize*, *fuck* is like *kick*—
                        though languages change.
Even English might, if we said to our spouses
fuck you, meaning may our false dawn coruscate
with wheeling galaxies while wood thrushes
flute us an aubade. If we told the tired toll booth clerk,
fuck you, may your beloved speak your name
like the prayer it is. If I could say to you, reading this,
let your delight lift the hairs of the very mountains;
may the road, or something, rise always up
to meet you; let your conjugations star the endless
ice-night of July on the slopes of Mount Erebus
with beeswax votives, and may it be so for all the billions,
even the petty, even the cruel: *fuck you, and fuck us all*.

The change

The warm hormones, the hot soup and sweet tea
we were willing to feed others first, wanted
to feed others first, grow first cold, then mold-
coated, crusting the cauldron that'll later be clean
as bone. The hot bath of abnegation pours
slowly down the drain into the dark, becoming septic.
Ovary-opiates have run their course
in long-medicated blood, final dregs
flushed away, till we can no longer believe
we don't need what we need, what you need
is more important, someday there will be time
for what we need: there is today but no someday,
not for crazy cat ladies beginning to eat cats
or turn to cats themselves, natural-born killers.
Though we may do what you ask, now you have to ask.
Antennae turned to catch your wish
before you wished it are furled now, clean
laundry in a locked drawer. Like werewolves,
skins creeping at the eastern horizon's first
pewter moongleam, we begin to become and believe
ourselves, transformation we cannot stop,
for which we will never be forgiven,
we are bitches now, cat bitches, wolf
bitches, we must be shunned and killed, and we will.

The Earth Witch of Colchis

Medea remembers the sheep

Sheep took a while—thirteen thousand
years, including millennia
after Mesopotamians
began on domestication:
the gathering of soft under-
fleece from briar and branch and thorn,
the capture of the wild mouflon,
the breeding lines for deeper calm,
plucking the soft loose wool by hand,
until greed came, and, so, shearing.
Each dingy sheep in every field,
its ragged tail crusted with shit,
its pink skin shivering with wind,
is royal, heir to the long line
of heritage which made mutton,
merino, black ram sacrificed
to make an old man young again.
Each browses the confluence line
of chance and choice, nature and craft.
Even an ordinary ewe
is marvelous, for those who see;
each pulled and pilled Goodwill sweater
offers the miraculous warmth
grown by beasts and worn by man.
Right at the start, I should have asked
what more he wanted, why plain wool
wasn't wonder enough, why he
had to have a fleece made of gold.

Medea names herself

> *Everything you are, everything you do,*
> *everything you have comes from the earth.*
> —NICK CARTER

I gave him the world because I
am world made flesh. This world, holy
grail, ace of cups over-brimming
with rivers of freshwater fish
and freshwater love, sweet quinoa,
mountains of platinum, orchards
of pomegranate made fertile
by the singing glories of bees.
Who else could offer a man wealth
without end, plus love, glory, lore,
babies, and a sheep robed in gold?
who else can add in miracle
and magic, can brew up new youth
for a man's withering father
in her copperpot stew, who speaks
in the tongues of lark and cock?
Only a woman of the world,
a world that is a woman too,
a woman who's inside the world
that always offered everything.
But he couldn't embrace the gift
of grace, or take the time to praise
and wonder; Jason had to think
it was his due. He's every man
who ever wed the beautiful
high-earning loving strong and kind
to see if he could, then moved on
to his next whim, casually grabbed
for something new: master, owner,
late-stage capitalist of love.

But a world is too big to own.
He needed someone he could be
bigger than, a girl like plastic
bobbing upon a vast ocean
of seabirds and menhaden shoals,
a sweet alliance, one more snug
cunt, and then one more, yet one more.
Maybe because he played pocket
pool through high school ecology,
he never saw the connections.
He thought that when you cool lead rods
in groundwater, only other
people's children die. Thought you can
take everything a world can give
and burn it to hot rock and still
somehow there's air for you and yours
somehow your wife will still make bread,
somehow you get to keep the kids.

But how could you kill the kids?

Medea answers

How could the caged rabbit reabsorb the unborn kits.
The dog in labor eat the threatened pups.
The refugee axe the cat
to save it from starving when she flees.
How could your plastic bag choke a loggerhead.
How lightningstrike meet global warming drought
and flare the tumbleweed into a wheel of fire
rolling across the innocent plain.

—Innocence, vengeance, forgiveness,
unforgiveness: stop your yap,
what's any of that to do with me.
I'm the honeybee pulling nectar from glyphosate-
laden goldenrod, and I'm the homeowner
who thought goldenrod too messy,
and I'm the bee-sisters dead in my thousands,
rigid-tongued. I'm the place
where the source of the everflowing
spring meets the slurry pit's seep. Convergence
point: effect and cause, choice
and chance and result, unalterable law. I'm just
what comes next when everything touches everything.

When Abraham ties his boy to the stone
and then asks God how could you,
like what's a guy supposed to do.
When Jason asks how could I,
while he plans his next war
like there are no hungry kids where his troops
will salt the furrows, like not one
of his men ever raped a little girl. I'm just
the one thing that leads to another.

I'm the world that gave birth to the kids
you've locked in the cage you built
with the lock my boline hacks free.
Those kids are the lucky ones.
Their troubles are done.
Don't talk to me about the kids.

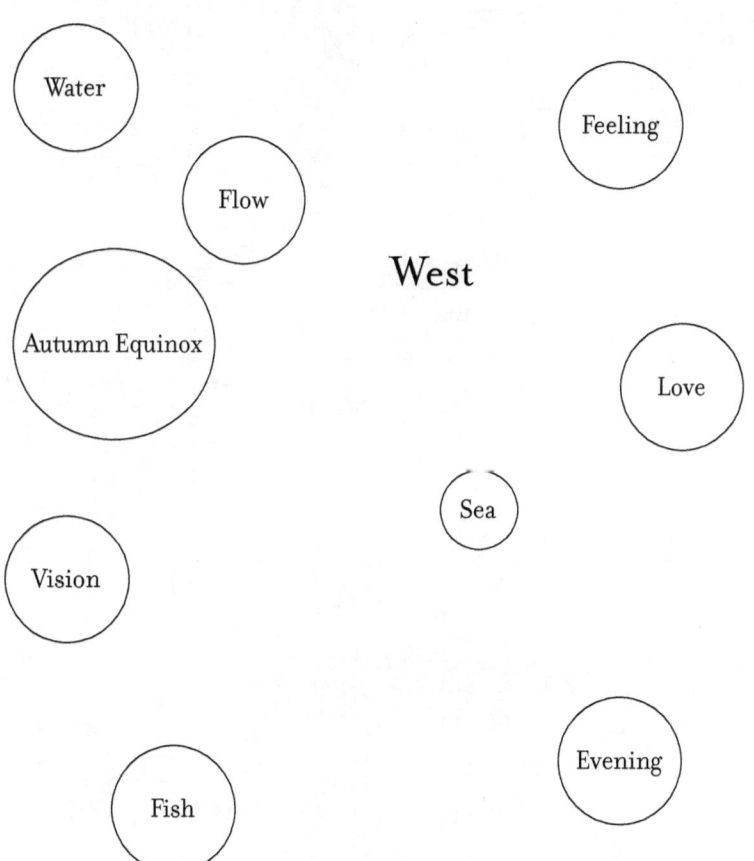

Applesauce on the equinox

She slices the flesh across the star
at the heart, cuts it into the pot,
tosses core and seeds into the pail
where they rest a while on their way
back to dirt. Not quite a crone
yet, nor a hag, though she too is on her way
back to dirt, she is bent, but quick
and sure with her black-handled knife.
Up from her kettle full of the fruits
of knowledge and death hisses
cinnamon-sweet steam, whispering
like escaping souls; she stirs
and blends as the sauce grows
slow and hot, as fumaroles smack
up thick apple-bubbles and suck
them back down. These atoms' path
from sunfire to mold is almost run.
Before they'll be young again
they must sink into this brew, stew
together, make their way into animal
bellies and animal warmth and thence
down into sand and soil, down
into earth-fire, dirt-sugar,
lava-juice, until hair-roots pry apart
each grain to drink them up
once more into blossom and bole to feel
that newnesss again, relearn all the words
of earth bright and fresh
as petals, minnows, fingerling salmon.
The apples are almost ready
to go. They cringed from the cauldron
at first, but now they know
what she is doing, what she is making
of them, how they will be

lost and forgotten and transformed
and reborn from the black pot, the hot
clear jars, the stove-fire that is the heart
and heat of the world.

Fat

Up here how it drags
at you, cleaves to earth,
sin of flesh never forgiven
by anyone who claims the right
to forgive. But in the sea it shines sleek
as a seal, strong as a whale, here fat
is float as you suck your breath
of snorkel-air and plunge
through bottleglass-green to the trove
of sand where just as you begin
to focus your blinking eye

on the rubble of crumbled shell
and pebble, the ground-garnet glitter
of possibility—up, up
again, no kick can keep you down
as you pop to the surface, a cork float
in the salt, your heavy meat
turned to ascent incarnate.
Fat! you snarl,
bobbing on the sea-skin
like a basking shark, lighter
for once than you desire.

But the real sharks, how they eye you
up, ogle those tender folds
and rolls as their warmth burns away
inside you to stave off the chill
of the heaving depths, its alien
un-density lifting you back
to breath: their cold eyes see
what you are. What they want.
They would take you any day,
savor each succulent ounce, they know
how rich and sweet you really are.

Ode: Slime

Nasal caves and crevices and hollows pour
slippery liters each day. Sluice
out the sinuses and see what swims free,
yellow plaques, blocked blood, gray air's flecks
of grime, all borne out on the limpid stream
of slime, the goblet cells' pure wine.
And then the bowels, the bronchi, the eyes,
each shawled in its fine caul of slime.
When we cry out, convulsed by delight,
or weep till we can't breathe,
what marks release but long slick gouts
of slime? And we barely compare
to the frogs, the eels, the slugs whom slime
lets climb the inimical world, the hagfish
or slime eel, all those kin
with whole skins filmed in that soft shine,
or the algaes or the zombie worms
designed wholly from slime, for the holy
mucus, this bright ooze, is how this world runs
and breathes, how living things move.

And what about beyond, out there
where most of *what is* can't be seen?
Don't you wonder if those outward-hurling stars
aren't carried like burning grains
on something? if everything that ever
was isn't flowing, forever,
perhaps through some divine
cavity draining who knows
where? if all that old night and dark
matter, star-speckled, aren't really hyaline
transgalactic tributaries irresistibly running,

transparent as time, toward some strangely
lubricious space-black sea, so clear
we look right through them, glittering
rivers of heavenly slime?

Pre-menopausal red-tide death-period arrives while I walk with parents along Chesapeake beaches

Welling. Seeping. Dashes to cover
of cattails, reed-fringe, open woods,
grass-grown-over logging roads,
leaving rags and strings of DNA
to sink into silt, dissolve
into decay, reach down to roots
and up into grass, join
in red wedding with the mud-
making bacteria, feed the future's
hollow spathe-leaved reeds and so flow
into what immortality this flesh
can know, built on its foundation
of sand, these parents' ageing
flesh. The clumps and clots
look strange in sunlight, released
from their cave-dark for daylight
to turn wine-black to sudden ruby,
raspberry, pomegranate's
crimson-purple, bright blots
in the clean sand baptizing
this homeplace with woman-
blood, witch-blood, marking
these long shores' doorposts
with thick sigils telling death, yes,
yes, all right, we're coming,
but today we're no bloodless
shades beyond their broad
tidal creek, I still bleed mortal
blood: so pass, pass by this time.

Aphrodite Ourania

Some gods want blood,
a cock throat-slit,
a neck-wrung dove,
a man burnt alive in a wicker cage.
Those gods are always near.
Ares drinks madness, rage,
a hecatomb of fear;
Hephaistos, careful work;
art's labors slake his thirst.
And the god of love?
All of the above.
She'll take words
sung on lyres—let the liars sing!
—she'll take years of mute
service, she'll let you rave,
nor will she refuse blood.
But love is foam-born, shining
like the evening
star on the semen-
bitter sea; salt smears her bright hands,
which is why tears are
her first, her best, her truest offering.

Ode: Erections in sleep

The moon sinks toward the westward
mountains outside the cold glass; tree
shadows stretch a scant inch; inside, in bed,
the tide of morning slides upstream
through the elastic veins that feed the quiet
flesh pressed to your back, gradually fills
their blue walls like estuarine streams
inexorably pushed by bay, till the still
pause at the flood's crest before the blood
tide turns and sinks to follow the pull
of the moon back to the belly's deeps.
Later, as you lift and fall on swells
of dream, the same salt flush rises
once more, a mist on the face of the waters,
going only where it's always come
and gone, leading nowhere but back
into sleep, no curl and crash on marsh
or sand, a living flow, a slow, sweet neap.

Mountain brook lamprey

Ichthyomyzon greeleyi

Lambere, to lick, *petra,* stone.
Among your own, you're lambent,
flickering, licking creek floors like old-
gold tongues or slender fingers;
secretive stone-sucker, your larvae
light dim mucus-tube lamps
in the silty ooze below the rapid riffles.
Sand-eater, algae-skimmer,
ecosystem engineer filtering and tilling
bright air into streamy substrates,
you're no parasite
like your great seagoing kin;
you lack the cachet of horror,
lack even the jawless mouth-
gear, the grating teeth, until you
change—and then, adult, you don't eat
at all, let alone drink blood.
Your tiny hagfish maw
clutches only stones, shaping
shallow nests for your spawn;
maturity is only for love, brief
delight sliding over into death
easy as a lamprey
through water, as light through glass.

And none knows your numbers,
or what *stream* will mean
when they're dammed into zeroes
round as a buccal funnel.
Secret-keeper, that rasp-
file mouth shapes no sound,
tells us nothing. If you go,

you'll go with no word,
sucking at the stone
of silence as if it held all secrets,
all the slippery lives past and to come.

The color of aquamarine: a spell for blessing

Pale beryl cousin of emerald, whose name
means *seawater*. Color of light
through suspended solution of salt, milt,
urine, single-celled cyan algae,
fringed baleen, elastic frayed
from someone's bikini; of salt-crusted
pearls' gritty sheen lodged in oysters' soft
whole-body labia or in puckered octopus
suckers; of seafloor ley lines
throbbing with the underpinning pulse
of lava and radiating jade
haloes of energy for those who can see
with the slotted eyes of the squid,
sharks' ampullae of Lorenzini,
the lateral lines of traveling
toadfish, or gannets' plunging flanges.
Color of turquoise, if turquoise could be thin
and clear. Color of seawater, that solution
of absolutely everything: color
I choose to spin
out from the frontal lobes into which
I have called it with memory—
out in words and the stir
of fingertips, through the electromagnetic caul
of this body, to wrap it around you
as a shieldwall against malice
and harm: electrical, unseen, blue-
green, aquamarine.

Copperheads in heaven

Someone I loved used to kill
copperheads with a shovel's
sharp blade, the same old fear,
the same old waste.
And if the copperheads are anywhere
now, he is there too.
If I thought of heaven
I would think of a place
where there is a place
for everything. Everything
driven from here would end
there, no matter who
killed whom: sanctuary.

In heaven, then, perhaps
the soft sky flashes,
riven with passenger pigeons;
and heaven's creeks flicker
with Maryland darters and foam
with the spawning shad;
and in the south of heaven
Taino is spoken aloud
in an afternoon rain;
and maybe he, nearly
young again now,
lifts his broad-eared head
to a flight of Carolina parakeets
as he sits on the dock he built,
and the copperheads sleep
by his feet on the windworn boards
in the tender autumn sun.

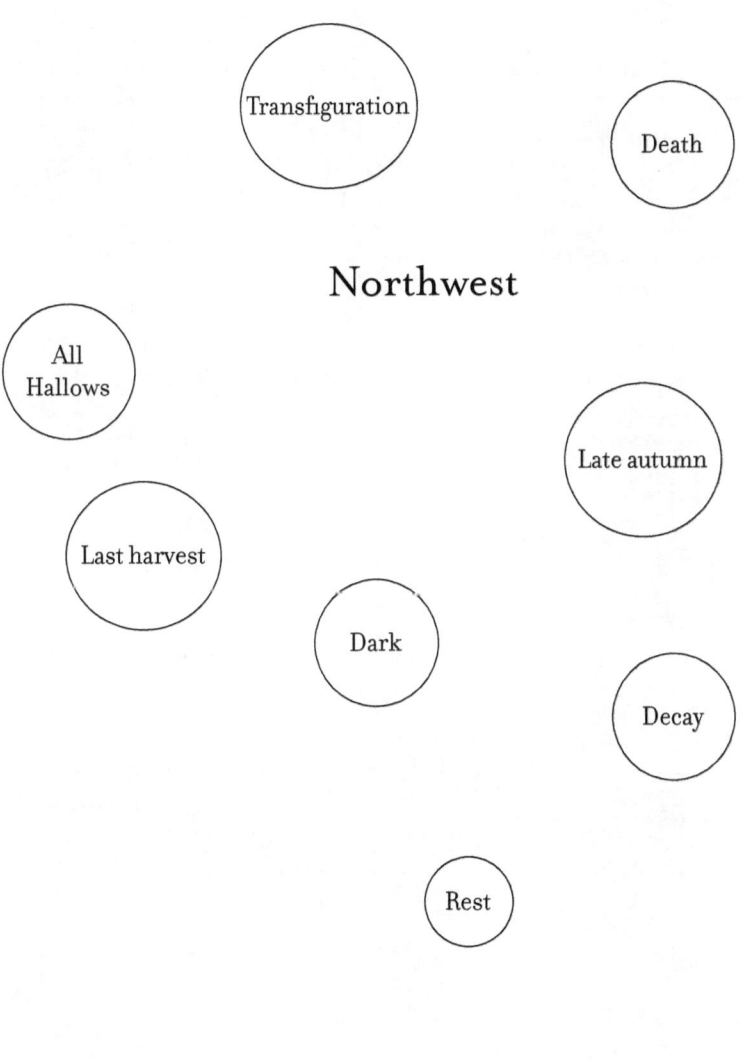

Four goldenrods

All through the drought, these four
goldenrod stalks were dauntless,
lifting aloft their feathery gold
and amber scepters, inclining their heads
like monarchs when the summer
wind stirred their harsh leaves. No thirst
could make them droop or despair:
noblesse oblige, they seemed
to whisper. *We must be strong*
for the piped rhododendron leaves'
dry leather, for the noons
when even the beautyberries droop.
But now in the fall's first great
rain, now they can surrender,
now they lean toward the soaked earth
and brush their faces against it,
they bend their strong spines in arches
fit for cathedrals, bow
their heads, lay down their crowns.
After such need, there is no joy
like leaning to receive, accepting grace
with grace, with the whole
body, the whole life, offering up
all their pride and strength.
They kneel all day in their beatitude;
they weep clear tears of relief,
and in the field beyond,
all the star-white and iolite-blue
asters do the same, shaping springy stems
into long curves and clouds of thanks-
giving, like the faithful at their truest
prayers. Longing could not
touch them like gratitude.

Things to love about the rain

What it does in headlights: water-streaks plunging through the beam flash out that gold gleam like they've been waiting all their tiny lives, or their endless lives. Like water loves light, waits ready to praise it every second, every time. How the headlights seen through rain waver and glimmer, long lines of bright quivering. As if everyone could be warm and safe in the chilly gray.

How it softens the tough earth: if the dead want to come back, now is when. They wait for the rain to return, to speak in trickles, hisses, whispers.

Windows and windshields: lucid brief jewels tremble the windshield into clear oval waterlights, glass trickling past glass, the quick liquid sliding over the slow. The first spattered lines across a window, how they gather weight, round into droplets then drops, pulled again toward their path through earth.

How it doesn't have to come for weeks, years, ever. Grace you can't make, can't earn, can't force. Ignores guns, uniforms, laws, bribes, words. Say *please:* the rain won't hear. Won't hear if you say *thank you, thank you,* though you say it anyway because you can't not, because it bubbles through your tongue like seeps from the hill.

The shine it puts on the dry world. Harsh concrete cracked black asphalt sparkling and running with rain, roads for a little while turned back to shallow creekbeds.

The voices it gives to gargoyles.

The domes and the bells, when children's umbrellas tip over into a faint, ribs up, to be filled with crystal cabochons and with flowers so small only the young see them, orchid tongues of henbit and deadnettle, veined petals of wild pansy.

How for those in need it may yet save everything, defer debts, feed kids, fill wells, raise streams, though often too much in deadly floods of mud, and usually too late.

The dapple-rings on the moving skin of river and creek, half-second-perfect circles intersecting the dozens of other half-second-perfect circles, not one seeking to be the only ring, each one crossing spreading rounding wider and thinner, all slipping down, downstream, away, now, now.

How it falls and falls on the mossy roof of the cabin on the mountainside deep in your mind, the place safe because no one knows where you are, despite there being no such cabin. How it gurgles in that roof's rusty gutters, sings in the downspouts, rings in the rain-chains, a woman humming alone in a house.

How it fills in your footprints, lets you be erased, washes you clean away.

Red beans

Before you begin, sauté the onions long and slow. Before that, dice them carefully, unhurrying. Before that, soak the kidney beans all through the night while you rest in your bed. When the onions soften and sizzle, add the green chiles, also sliced small. With them, the cumin seeds, toasted to fragrant and ground brown and fine with a pestle. All that makes the bed at the bottom of the crockery pot for the smooth maroon beans, in their turn a bed for clear water, without form and void, which they will thicken and change all the long day you're off speaking, teaching, simmering words: beds under beds, geologic strata to be tilted and turned by fire tectonics, tumbled by bubbles in God-troubled seas. Then macerated in stomach acids, split and pried down to molecules by hungry intestinal cells, recast from vegetable into animal, matter into energy, bean-seed and bean-soul cracked by the heat of a life it never planned. It's only dinner: only there is no only, dinner being chemistry biology energy transfer transfiguration twice over. Attend. Don't hurry. Dancing like Shiva, or the beans, in your circle of fire swinging its own circle round the sun, it is all right to take time, to eat well, to grind fine: for when you open the door from the cumin-scented warmth and walk out, perhaps with a nose-souled dog, there are the stars of autumn, shaken and tumbled in the cauldron of the void, and all around them, the dark waters are troubled.

Until the cows come home

I have been waiting a decade
and more, standing out in this now-
autumn pasture—same lightning-struck sassafras
standing warped and riven afternoon
after morning, winter after fall,
same tawny broomsedge feathering
seedpuffs into the wind—
straining for the distant clank
of cowbells. As evening lengthens
I tell myself the splotched shadow
under the far pine is a Holstein, black
paintsplash over dingy flanks,
that clump of broomsedge is a fawn
Jersey, dropping her wide ears to pull
fescue, and that burnt stump is a black
Angus calf, irritably switching his tail,
and that although they don't want me to know,
they are all ambling peaceably
toward me and toward the barn beyond,
though the east end of its roof
has fallen in and no clover
or alfalfa has sweetened its rotting
loft all the years I've stood here
waiting. Surely I see them now.
I can wait forever for cows,
as they waited once for their lowing calves
to be returned from the heavy trucks.
I can see anything, believe anything,
except that what will never
come again will in fact never come
again, that Buttercup and Bossy
and Bess are long gone to feedlot
and slaughterhouse, conveyor-
belt and hammerstroke, that neither you
nor those cows are ever coming home.

Elegy at All Hallows

I scoured this gourd's bright lantern clean
of gut and filament and slime
to light kids' way to chocolate bars'
soft waxy oversweetened bite;
but now the face is shrinking in,
triangular and fiery eyes
and cheerful double-pointed fangs
puckered into a parody
of petulance or grief, its long
grooves bending back toward the blank
emptiness I left at the core.
Wasted and shattered, all its kin,
or carted off to the landfill,
some few, perhaps, made into pies,
some few seeds burrowed into dirt;
possums will eat this one tonight,
its sugars bright in their red eyes
and in their shaggy silver hair.
But there are many darker ends
than to be scraped out and used up
for everything it has to give,
each seed devoured or scattered out,
and in the cavity that's left,
a melting stub of candle set
to drip and gutter in the breeze
that whistles through its sinking lips:
its mortal entrails useless now,
its cored-out hollow heart become
a bowl to pour out candlelight,
a lamp consumed by its own light.

Ode: Yeast

Here they are again. The yeasts which should be brewing
beer, raising bread, now set about digesting
and fermenting you, lifting rumpled fungal clusters
in the creases around toenails' plates of horn, dapple violet
or white on vulva or tongue, it doesn't matter
where, wherever it was, you thought it was yours,
not theirs, not choirs in which the fungi sing
mycelial exuberance clear as a thrush,
if you knew how to hear. But you don't,
not yet. Crop-dust with terconazole, miconazole,
slaughter the benign and the innocent
along with those you designate
to bear the weight of guilt: you will embrace
any poison to seize back your own
territories, colonies. But as those thick blossoms
writhe and shriek under napalm smears, pause
to wonder, with wonder: what if. What if
the zombie-ant fungus which scourges its host
into high places, to burst through its external
skull a fruiting body scattering spume
over new generations of ants, soon
to be fungal zombies themselves—is more than kissing
cousin to these more familiar kin. What if
you let them live, what hybrid self you'd become.
Whether, a month after you let leaven
flourish, you too might develop alien tastes
for ambrosia, Cosmopolitans, shots
of corn syrup, chocolate rice krispie treats,
offerings borne to your fungal overlords;
if as joints stiffen and organs stagger, ghostly fungus-
flowers, translucent in daylight, would begin to bloom
from nose, eyes, scalp, turn their stipes toward the dark
of the moon, flutter their delicately fleshy gills
to spurt spores colonizing first pets, then

spouse, then students in the classes
which by then you will have begun teaching
in near-darkness, presenting slide after strange
slide on mycology's seductive study, the endless
uses and virtues of the humble yeast: pale spirits of the dusk
and the dew, fermenters of wine, inheritors of the earth.

Sweet gum

Liquidambar styraciflua

On the sandy track, a smashed squirrel boils
up fresh maggots when stirred with a hand,
refuse of the same old haste and waste,
while the bright October wind sifts down
sweet gum leaves over gray fur and crushed
flesh, reminding the springing squirrel-
mind that black gum leaves turn red, and sweet-
gum leaves—hanging among their caltrop-
seeds—turn purply-black; but that's naming
for you, in a life where we learn late
or not at all, and at least sweet gum
smells sweet, amber-sap native of a new
world which was always the same old world:
bite the sandy stem of a fallen
star-shaped leaf and you'll catch myrrh-resin,
breathe up incense, even as you feel
its grit grate in your teeth and must spit
and spit. The same old world's full up
with those telling the same old story:
the one where rot sliding into the maws
of ivory worms is always more real
than the life that carried that squirrel here
on five-clawed feet, death never less than
appalling, the grit always harsher
than the sassafras-tang of the sap
is bright; where joy is so bourgeois
that they're ashamed to own the fine
of these few minutes standing on sand
beside the dead, to gnaw the gritty
stem of a leaf whose life has sunk back
into its tree. But today, strangely,
you remember that in this sudden

second, you can pause, you don't always
have to collude while that same old
story eats all the other stories,
that this wringing place has many names,
that another face of all the rage
and grief is praise. As these maggots praise,
curling like ecstatic toes in their first
first feast, refusing to waste anything.
As this gum tree praises, releasing
deep-purple five-pointed stars into
the shining morning, alligator-
barked being whose first name is *sweet*.

At 50, my brother who always hated children finds a daughter

> ... The present life of man upon earth ... seems to me in comparison with that time which is unknown to us like the swift flight of a sparrow through the mead-hall where you sit at supper in winter ... flying in at one door and immediately out at another ... safe from the wintry tempest, but after a short space ... he immediately vanishes out of your sight, passing from winter to winter again.
> —ST. BEDE, *Ecclesiastical History of the English People*, trans. A. M. Sellar

It's hard to doubt the mystery and the wonder of a world
where this brother and I can find ourselves gathering
sticks from the soft stubble of October grass outside the house
where we were raised up, here where we picked up sticks
for fifteen years, thirty years ago, and, the place being all
but woods even then, the sticks and the work all but endless,
always to be done anew; and where we can find ourselves now,
under the whistling of whitethroats returning for winter,
collecting sticks yet again, with the years folded and doubled
because this time it is with her, four-year-old Leia Hannah,
darting in for a hug and then out to grab up and juggle
sticks of which there are always, even now, more and more,
while yellow walnut leaves flicker and flutter down
through air clear as water was then, and in rays of autumn
sun, columns of translucent gnats spin and dance
their brief day of life in the long light.

This child has never been betrayed; she is as joyful
as she is new. Next year she will go to school, this sudden
daughter, luminous bloom on our generation's barren
limb, to learn cruelty, injustice, trouble. Feet
on the home sand, arms cluttered with a rubble
of twigs from the home walnut tree in the afternoon
of the shortening day, I say aloud—to no one,

since now Leia has abandoned the sticks and run
to blow soap bubbles—*this is the heart of the crystal,
star at the apple's core, this is it.* But
as an undulating bubble quivers past and strands
on an aster to tremble and slide rose-green prisms
over its shimmering side, *no,* I think now,
*this is the moment that ends as you touch it, gnat
in the last shaft of sun, sparrow two-thirds through the hall,
this is it, and it is the skin of the bubble.*

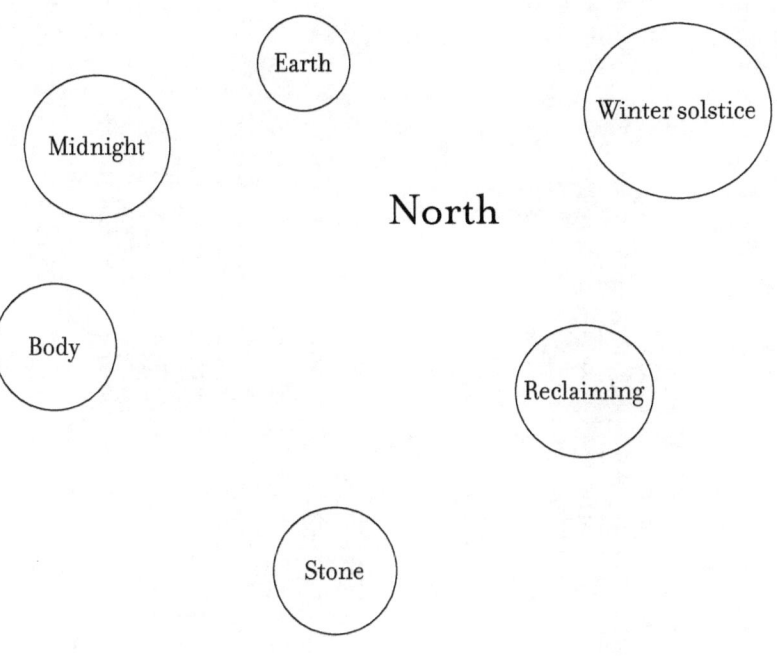

Winter solstice

At the top of the cove loop, the four-way crossroads—
sacred, if you think like that, to Hecate,
goddess of witches, doorways, secrets, the moon.
Passage over the culvert through which Fernshadow
bubbles and splashes down the groove of the cove.
Stand here a moment, bare tree among bare
trees, over water running under the south
of the earth, to see the morning sun low
in the brightening air, before you walk on to take
the road down the far side, before you come through
the door of winter turning on that hinge.

Crow cosmogony

The day we made the world, scattered
shattered sand across the deep
steeps and hollows of the sea,
we were playing with chance,
a stance few other gods admired.
We retired then from creation and let things
sing as they would, go
to whatever end luck called good.
We could, and did, breathe in a platypus here,
a shearwater there—evolution
our solution to dogma and fate,
the weight of always being in charge
of stars, shoals, plague, all that—
but by and large, we let go, let
sweat and thought fall away,
stray like questing possums
or blossoms of blown snow.
So it was. We didn't worry how
our sowing would grow. We went back
to hacking with our thick
black bills at death and waste, harrying
carrion, even as the dead
bled ever more numerous over the new
true-straight stone roads, here
where we shaped the bright turns
and returns of the world, invited
night in: do that, and you get
what you get. Despised
as flies, we pick through pale grass
for carcasses gone flat and dry;
we rise under your very wheels
from meals scant and cold, bring
strings of gut back to our young. But so

goes the world, when you let it go,
throw yourself in its rolling motion, chance
chance: we live on broken squirrels
in the world we made this way.

Ode: Anus

Asshole, they call you, lowest and darkest of the low and the dark, butt
of all jokes, mouth of the blast, vent for the Anglo-Saxon
fart and *shit,* hidden lip with no tongue:
there are few hymns to you, muscular and grave
and diligent anus, monastery novice faithfully shoveling
soil each day to channel away all we can't use,
simple-lifer, minimalist de-clutterer with more faith
and discipline than Marie or Martha, who also have
anuses. And though Dante crawled down Satan's haunch
toward a summoner's den of damned friars,
though Absalom kissed Alisoun's nether eye, neither
Dante nor Chaucer praised your keen feeling: neither
your deep exorcisms, your casting-out
of what possesses us so piercing that some have tiled
red pentacles round the base of porcelain toilet pedestals,
arcane stars to fence in what the bowel summons up
and what you, anus, put down, expelling Gothmog,
demon lord of the abyss, in exuberant relief
akin to that of the crow spattering white over newly painted
porch railings—no, nor your power of pain,
rending cramps, unzip-rip of the all-but-healed
fissure reducing even the strong to whimpers,
voiceless endurance of bees who die rather than defile
the hive, desperate anal vents locked tight. Freud
who also had et cetera et cetera thought art was feces
and money was feces but barely praised you,
organ of the creation of space, sacred rat
of black passages where, famously, no sun shines,
much-mocked unloved asshole, living ring
of muscle and nerve splitting wood, carrying water,
his holiness the abbot shitting in the withered field,
Zen of the letting-go, local god at the lintel
who opens the way from this second
into the next, the next, each second wholly
and inescapably its own here and now, each equally holy.

Happy light

It's made to make you glad
on dull cold days, keep you
from being seasonally affected, crying
over car insurance, imagining
flogging yourself with barbed
wire, leaving gouges brown
with rust, swelling with tetanus.
Full spectrum, mock sun. Maybe it helps;
surely it makes nothing
any worse. Until you realize
there's pressure. Even the lamp
is needy and anxious as a border
collie; it wants work
and reassurance. If you leave
it on while you go to lunch,
afterwards its white radiance
is trembly. It whispers *I shone
and shone and no one came,
no one saw! There was no one
to make happy. You! You're back!
Give my burning meaning.
Am I bright enough? are you happy
now? how about now?*
And you don't know what to say.
The light quivers like unfallen
tears. You sit still,
regarding the lamp like a dangerous
lunatic, as if you'd never heard
of barbed wire. You try to look happy.

The narrative of stones

A loose stone tries an assassination
in a talus-patch over Lost River:
rolls under a boot, seeks to pitch me off
the edge. It fails, being perhaps a young
stone, fresh from some local volcano, but
sends me stumbling into rocky canyons
of story, all the action and drama
of these stones' long lives. Born molten and poured
through underground runnels of fire, spewed
into air with force enough to rewrite
global climate, gabbro, scoria,
obsidian, basalt; or ground endlessly
by glaciers and borne on rivers of ice,
first slow as time and now trickling ever
faster; or beginning existence
as a scrim of river-silt compressed
together by the gravity-drag
of the whole world with a thin weed, a moth's
exoskeleton, sandstone, shale, crumbly
chalk, glacial conglomerate, cannibalistic
rock absorbing small brethren like amoebae;
or formed as some mountain's marrow-bone
before being cracked and split into crumbs
and chunks, pried loose, released, tumbled and spilled
down river after river on their long
road to the shifting floor of the spring sea:
their lives are all history and plot, change
rising from change, no character we blink-
and-gone meat-people are likely to read.
Walk along asphalt, crunch over gravel,
it's no life we can imagine, and yet—
from the cliff leaning over my shoulder,
the rubble crumbling under my soles,
the pebbled shoals of the blue-green stream's

bed far below—these rocks are rolling on
through story, and how they tell, how they speak,
how they sing it for those with ears to hear:
though their readers—even geologists,
translating one painstaking word a day
into sagas with no patience for such
temporary concerns as tragedy
or morals—are brief as breath, mayflies
alighting a second on the title
page of the Rig Veda because its
granite face has grown warm in the noon sun.

Ode: Falafel

for Jess

> . . . he said, If thou be the Son of God,
> command that these stones be made bread.
> —MATTHEW 4:3, KJV

Are those mossy rocks? she asked
without irony of the piled falafels,
lumpy, gritty, rich algal
green with their freight of parsley,
cilantro, dill. And so we saw
them a moment too: messy stream-
drawn stones transfigured into bread
of lunch, the dare Christ refused
in the desert accepted without fanfare
by the chickpea's fluttering lanceolate
leaf, the food processor's whirlyblur,
the water of this one earth. Algae-slimed
cobbles, massy weights of grain.
Brick shaped from minerals
and sunlight. Stone slab founded
on chickpeas' spilled marbles rolling
and scattering a dozen directions, random or not
random as the big bang's fling
of stars out into their burning
one-way courses. Rough protein wheels
turning and turning this world for seventy-
five hundred years and counting. Rock
which feels so firm under our hands
even as it goes endlessly hurtling
across the endless void, so solid
you could build a house on it,
a house with many rooms.

Cursive

A witch-general of the resistance, one of three
recruited from the mill's weaving-room after blueshirts
broke the last union, writes a dispatch in glyphs
only a witch can read, and even among witches, only
an old witch: the Palmer runes she learned a thousand
years ago when there were schools and she kicking
third-grade patent maryjanes on chrome rungs,
her bright black cornrows sparkling scarlet
and turquoise with beads. All along the way, at relay-
points for dromedary, caravan, carrier pigeon, boy
soldiers who have seen all the vids and plan
to die with a defiant smile, the young
seek to read the script, but no, only the one waiting
can decode it, before dropping back on her cot to die.
The young call it cursive; they think it carries
a curse, and maybe it does.
                       Only this story isn't true,
because secret writing is only a sideline: back in that long-
ago class, the witches learned to weigh things with scales.
Those boys who think they'll die bravely silent,
vital words knitted safe into scarves or knotted
into bootlaces, who in the end will beg and weep and piss
themselves: they have borne those boys, nursed
them. And the glass slivers under the nails,
the witch-waking, the water never brought:
they have borne those too. No one
would recruit these women to turn kids
over to war, not when in the pans
of their hands they have borne
those lives' weight. Their measure. Their worth.
Those witches are still back in the clack and roar
of the plant, breathing lint, winding bobbins, snipping
threads. They have been all along.
Their curses will never be heard.

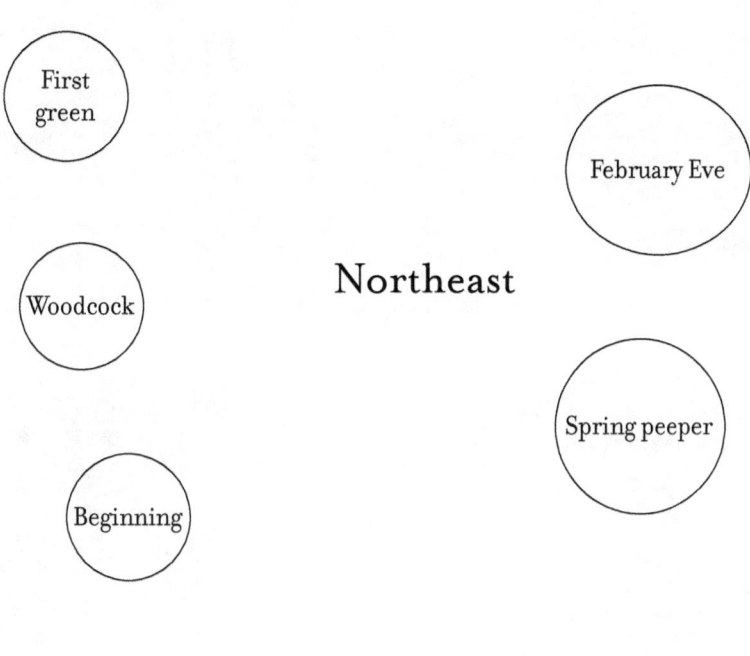

Pink red gold orange iridescent scarf

for Devon

This moment when I glance
down at this silly carnival-
colored scarf, slender strand
that warms only the eye—
its artful scatter of eyelash
yarn scarlet as a mandarin dragon,
those goofy gold ribbons stuttering
among fuchsia organzas (cobweb
ladders to absolutely nowhere
you can see), the woolly cotton-
candy rickrack and the shimmers
of iridescent tangerine—and it catches
the saw-raw March wind and flutters
like confetti: this second
is the reason some crazed knitter
or seamstress conceived
this scarf, imagining
what she couldn't see, hope
of change toward better.
This scarf is sheer
glitter, thrust up
frivolous as a pink tulip
thrust through the cold
stolid clods of all our winter
days, this second, this day,
bearing its roseate ovary up
through the killing frost.

Red onion slices, salad bar, city hotel

You perfect cross-
section of rose-madder
rings around translucent
white around amaranthine
violet and so on and on, the blazing
lights raising your pure glisten
and gleam; you magnetic
fields wavering around common
center of lemon-peel daisy-heart
gold; you unpeeling layers
of meaning, which at their core
are still more pungent
onion, entirely and inevitably
yourself, more biting eye-
water, more volatilized
sulfuric acid, pyrrhic defense
in a long-since-lost rear-guard action—
in this concrete cavern your beauty
and defeat strike the eye with stringent
stings of greeting, your Kandinsky-
concentric circles—ringing their pith
like raindrop-haloes here
in a room where no rain
falls—just irregular enough
to testify you were once alive
in the earth which here is ground
beneath vast concrete slabs,
that you swelled with the honey
of the sun. If your life
had not plunged into this steel
tray, you might have made a poultice
to open clogged lungs, or softened
a long stew, and if left to shrivel
on a shelf, even now

that life in you would still
have tried one more time, thrust
out a royal-purple stalk
from a heart straining
toward sunlight.
              —Onion,
I don't know what either of us
is doing here, but I'll do my best
for us both. Today I'll drive
away from this place on the hard
and sparkling road back to dirt:
come into me, and I'll bring you
back there. Enter the wet cave
and dark cauldron of this mouth, infuse
this breath with your burning
spirit, let your crisp flesh be broken
on teeth and tongue. Heal me, become me,
give me courage, help me weep.

The rivers run through you

when it's dark enough, listen:
you can hear the invisible streams
flowing through the world and through
you: night wind brushing over the ridge
of the hill and through the window screen
into ear canal nostril lung blood
all the unseen rushing over you, into you:
nitrogen oxygen viruses micro-motes
of dust water vapor microwaves ultraviolet
bee-guiding stripes on the throats of marsh
marigolds whispers of the dead and the never

to be born, Jupiter's ghost-blue light
the cold radiance of the larval firefly
devouring envenomed prey in a communal
late-night buffet with a dozen of its kin:
all of it the night moving
in your branches and you a tree of this world,
thin xylem sucking thread-seeps of water
and energy, you: energy's leafcrowned channel
from sky to earth streambed for the lightning's
bursting burning river. This is the literal
truth: all of it running through you now

in through tongue and eyes and skin
and breath transforming as you read
to currents of outgoing air clear creeks
of urine flooding out of you again
into the air breathed up by screech
owl and water oak and your own
envenomed species-mates to the septic
tank and out through the drain field

into the obscure from which it sprang
and as it rills through you on its quivering
skin glimmers the bubble of your life
your life your just this now life

Choptank bluegills take part in the creation of the world

You couldn't say bluegills create the stream.
Torn from the stream, they choke
on blazing air. And yet. Those nests,
those few dozen shallow divots together
pocking the creek bottom in dimples
rich with sunfish generations: changing
creekbed, reshaping foundation.
That steady fan-flow of air-
bearing water over eggs settled among
the pebbles, ever so slightly changing
the river's braiding and unbraiding. That labor
of life: the work to work
with the current as it is and yet
to change it just enough, to manifest
a place a little better for bluegills, co-creating
the world in concert with oxygen exchange,
tectonic motion, that smashed and gash-
edged hubcap pinning down an immortal
plastic bag, the gravity of the moon, whirligig
beetles inscribing creek-skin with runes
written in water, whatever God you say. Flood
of protestors in the street's torrent, choking
on blazing air. A woman stirring cut
onions over heat, changing them just enough
to turn their burning tears to something
a little more sweet. Fingers moving the pen, the keys,
the lever, and the air and ground
of our lives ever so slightly shifting
in response, recreated (ever so slightly) anew.
The fearful fact: it matters what you do.

Black wool coat on a hook

It hangs so quietly, its lines straight and still:
nothing to see here, if you forget
that like everything, it's the headlight
of an endless tale-train, the vanishingly
sharp point of a mile-long pencil stiff with story.
Behind belted back and flared skirt: overseas
factory, shears and pattern, women with distended
bladders pedaling whirring needles, fear
of fire always at the door. Behind that, weaving
room, then dye room, the reek of the mordant
to set the black fast, the tumor-tasting air, the gone
union jobs. Back of that, spinning and carding
and fulling rooms, human lungs thick with lint.
Further, the slow adventures of sheep: oily
fleece under the shears, slotted pupils. Shearing
efficient and gentle, or slashes on the shivering
flesh. Crouch of the herding hound. Spring young,
kept to rear or taken for Easter, to wash
their devourers in the blood of the lamb.
Before that again, the grass, springy clumps
of March, vivid green flutters in the cold wind
beneath the pouring river of sunlight, blaze
of the star whipping in her own wind as her galaxy drags
her headlong toward Virgo.
    The coat hangs on the hook,
pulled toward earth by weight of sheep,
throbbing backs, vats of dye, pastures of grass.
If you look, sun shines through its close-
woven warp, sun which will one
day collapse into itself, turning first white
as a washed sheep, then in the end quiet and black
as a wool coat: the one you lift and slip on, as you walk out
into the March wind. Wrapped in and insulated by unseen
lives. Buttoned into the whole world, and beyond.

www.ingramcontent.com/pod-product-compliance
Lightning Source LLC
Chambersburg PA
CBHW020857160426
43192CB00007B/962